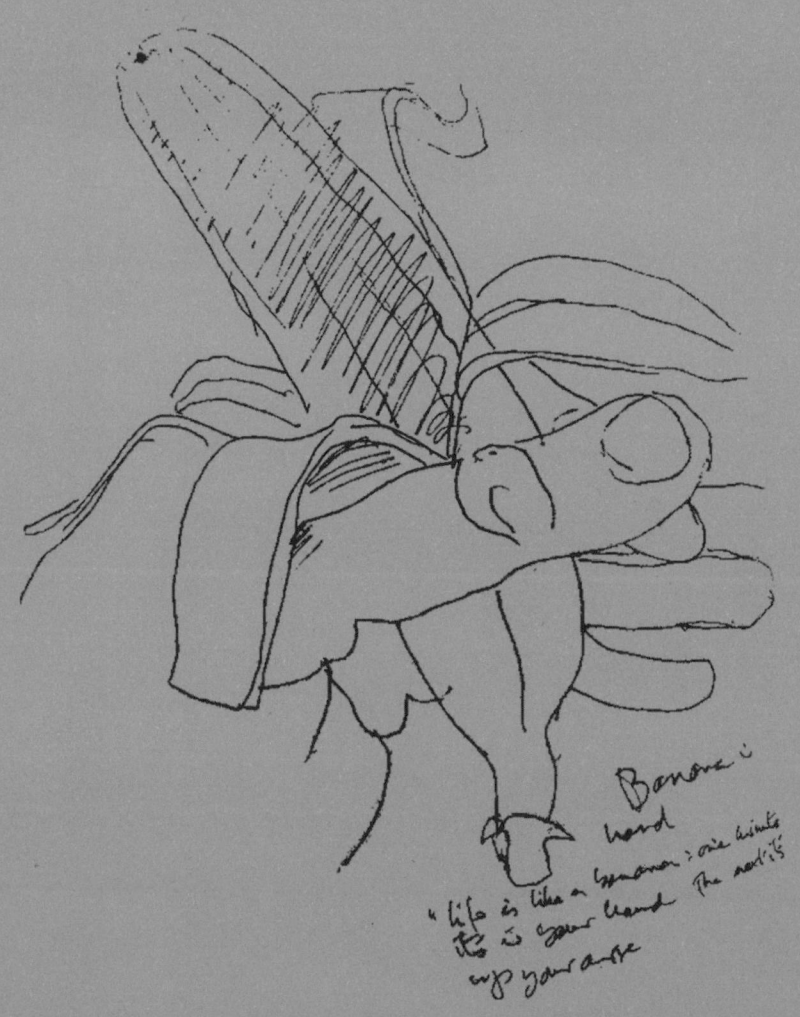

LIFE IS LIKE A BANANA

LIFE
is like a banana

Tony Wilson

Foreword by
Sorrel Pitts

Anthony Eyre
Mount Orleans Press

ACKNOWLEDGEMENTS

I would like to thank my publisher Anthony Eyre, for his patience and kindness; Sorrel Pitts for her hardworking professionalism in curating this selection from my 237 sketch books; and finally Grace Pilkington for believing in me from the very beginning of this project.

Published in Great Britain in 2024
by Anthony Eyre, Mount Orleans Press
23 High Street, Cricklade SN6 6AP

https://anthonyeyre.com

© Tony Wilson 2024

Tony Wilson has asserted his right under
the Copyright, Designs and Patents Act 1998 to be identified
as the author of this work.

ISBN 978-1-912945-50-4

A CIP record for this book is available
from the British Library

All rights reserved. No part of this book may be reproduced or transmitted
in any form or by any means, electronic or mechanical including
photocopying, recording or by any information storage
and retrieval system, without permission from
the copyright holder in writing.

Set in 12/16pt Joanna Nova

Printed in Malta by
Gutenberg Press

Pat reading

I wonder what happenings, excitements and thrills will be recorded in this book:— it's 90 pages await.

Foreword

In February, 2023, I received an email from a lady named Grace Pilkington. She had found my details online and was approaching me, she said, with an 'unusual request'. An elderly author called Tony Wilson was looking for an editor to curate some diaries he had been writing since the 1980s. They were, she said, 'rather amazing – philosophical musings and beautiful watercolour illustrations'. Grace had worked with Tony on a previous book, but as she lived in Hastings and he was in Wiltshire, she felt he needed to find someone local to curate the diaries. 'Are you available and would you be interested?' she asked. 'There are rather a lot of them.'

Intrigued by this description, I agreed to meet with Tony in his home in the lovely old village of Turleigh near Bradford-on-Avon. I found a gentle, funny and extremely intelligent, but very frail man who seemed to be surrounded by a lot of warmth and care. As well as the constancy of those he lives with – his grandson, Oliver, and Jack Russell, Rufus* – he is visited regularly by friends, cleaners, gardeners, and his devoted carer, Vanessa.

After an introductory chat, Tony sent me up to his office. I pulled out a small number of the carefully indexed diaries and immediately saw what Grace meant. The sketches and watercolours were striking in their simplicity and brevity, as was Tony's ability to reflect a mood or moment with just a few well-struck lines. I was also taken by his bold and often experimental use of colour and tone. In addition to the sketches and watercolours there were many writings – most were occupied with Tony's life with his wife Pat and their large family and group of friends, but others concerned his observations on life, reflections on historical events and – his favourite subject – what makes society function. It is this latter preoccupation that provided the subject matter for his previous two books – *The Universe on a Bicycle* (Elliot and Thompson 2007) and *The Wheels of Society* (Quartet 2021), which received glowing reviews in the *Daily Mail* and the *Times Literary Supplement* respectively.

Anthony Wilson did not initially seem destined to become an artist or philosopher. He was born in Ireland in 1931 and studied economics at Trinity College, Dublin, qualifying as a chartered accountant before becoming a financial controller. In his career, he worked for Price Waterhouse, the Avon Rubber Company, GKN and British Oxygen. In 1989, Tony moved to Turleigh with Pat. They had three children, Philippa, Mark and Luke, and five grandchildren – Oliver, Oscar, Freya, Freddie and Theo. Family members and the residents of Turleigh (who like to get together each year to make cider) are featured in the diaries along with Tony's beloved dogs, a bearded collie called Tilley, and Rufus.

It is clear from the diaries that Tony does not like to sit still for very long. His life has packed with interests and hobbies, including rowing (he was President of Bradford-on-Avon Rowing Club), sport, politics, writing, philosophy, sculpture and painting. His house is full of his sculptures and painting and as we chatted he pointed out that even the coffee table next to me had been carved by his own hand. Tony has had six solo painting exhibitions and his work was shown in the RA Summer exhibition in 1987.

Tony also loves to travel. When Pat was alive, they spent 10 weeks of every year in the tiny village of Simena in southern Turkey. There he sketched and painted the various local people and places he came to know and love. Despite suffering a disabling fall in November 2022, Tony has since returned to spend time in Turkey.

Tony has requested that the pictures and writings should appear chronologically (which at times may give them a random feel) and 'warts and all', with no embellishment or erasing of mistakes or other writings that have leaked into the image boundary. As AI creeps into our world, he believes there will be a strong drive towards 'authenticity' and would like this book to be part of the latter.

Getting to know Tony and curating this book for him has been one of the most rewarding jobs I have ever had and I only hope that I have done his talents justice. The selections I have made attempt to capture his rich inner life as well as the one he lived outwardly. They include deeply personal (often painful) thoughts about bereavement, aging and death, comic observations about the world and other people around him (Tony loves to people watch) and his concerns about the political state of the world. The artworks brilliantly capture village people as they go about their ordinary business, and the changing seasons and how they affect the landscape. Most of all, I hope the work demonstrates (as reflected in the TLS quote on the cover) how constant application and practice can lead to mastery of a craft even at a very late age. Tony Wilson is an inspiration to us all.

Finally, the selections covered in this book begin in 1998, but Tony actually started keeping diaries back in 1989. One wonders what other treasures might be found inside those pages!

Sorrel Pitts, June 2023

*Sadly Rufus died during my time curating the diaries. He is still mourned by Tony, Oliver, Vanessa and the residents of Turleigh, who preferred to call him 'Poofus' due to the random toilet donations he liked to leave around the village.

Prison with the constant sound of waves A METAPHOR FOR AMERICA

There is a lady here. She is dumpy & grey haired
She walks briskly round the compound every morning
(while Nella the incredible is playing Tennis)
round & round she goes round the pool round behind the Tennis court
for about half an hour
She wears a white T shirt
and dark blue Shorts
Yes but what is she doing?
Obviously she's been told it's good for her
to take exercise like this & walking is the best exercise
but why not out along the beach or somewhere nice?
She walks around inside the Condom Compound
like in a prison — just like it
What must be going on in her mind
That's where one's best thoughts come — out walking
but round & round the Condom Compound?
Have we come to this.
The fad for exercise combined with the fear of have-nots

So that
The only
Sensible
Solution
is a
daily walk
for 30 minutes
round & round
inside
The Condom
Compound

The last palm tree "Sunday's palm"

This is a metaphor for America: She has the money, the freedom,
the education, but this is how she ends up: in her own prison

Actually I've met her briefly and she seems to
be a very nice lady

AM I confirmed yesterday with Both Kemal and Esin that Islam is indeed v. simple. There is nothing in ritual or belief deeper than the 5 principles. There are many cults & sects like people who flagellate themselves & the whirling dervishes but nothing more at the centre. There is lots a bar to behave but nothing to match Christianity's commercialism, sex, torture.

Friday was a public holiday in Turkey. May 19th 1919 was the start of Ataturk's Turkish rebellion against the great powers. So lots of Turks have taken the long weekend off. Kemal the 2nd hand bookseller and Juliet also Esin and a party of 2/3 families — all at Salih's also the doctor a 35 yr old Turkish woman on his own. Lots of day tripper boats loaded up with Turks & parties of school children.

What really 'frightens' me is that

I never before really thought about the actual meaning of these words & ideas. I knew Christianity was nonsense & potentially evil but the fact that we accept this commercialisation is frightening. & to worship a god whose son padded about in a loincloth in the desert while we live in pre sodden house is farcical

it'll end in tears

6.11.00

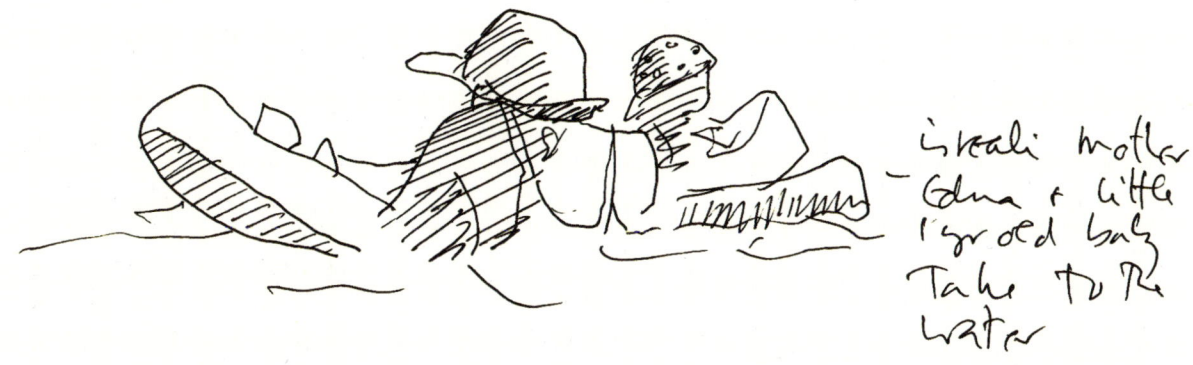

Israeli mother Edna + little 1 yr old baby take to the water

Stalmark x. Memet Tuli

Morality

I believe people are able to construct semantic complex structures which they don't really understand and that the history of philosophy is riddled with them — many/most of them nonsense. Hume, Descartes, Leibnitz, Kant, Wittgenstein. One might be able to prove this!

Zen & the art of M'cycle maintenance is riddled with these.

The current issues of the American scientist have very relevant book reviews: on the language of maths etc.

The descriptions — or attempts to describe — the universe in terms of 11 dimensions (see Summer '0, American scientist or scientific American) is a great example of this I have to day I get lost after 1½ pages or less but I suspect its nonsense a modern day example of medieval descriptions of angels

※ Cross paintings could be framed by backing them onto some material — patterned material. or even in plain see-through glass! That might be the best of all.

To accommodate glass have slip site edges board which extends under canvas.

|Mosquitoes|

Today's clever idea is for preventing mosquitoes. You simply train a pet bat: it would live by your bedside and in exchange for your feeding it with insects it would eat any mosquitoes that are bothering you. being related to mice and being social animals I'm sure they are intelligent and easily trained. Maybe they could do other jobs as well — not sure what yet.

Thick section maybe see-through or with writing behind! ie. blow-up sketchbook extracts. or copy the writing onto clear see-through film.

uli is brown as a berry after 2 wks

Uli

Karen

Philosophy asks the questions Science provides the answers Religion = too difficult 57

Bike ride.

① Asking the right question — or even asking questions at all. That is what PHILOSOPHERS do best. They ask questions that may never ever produce an answer. What else could one train a bat to do is a good example. It's the sort of question that might lead to a major breakthrough!

② It's a pity E.O. Wilson didn't include a chapter on cooperation in his wonderful book "The Diversity of Life" it would have been a winner

Bats could surely be trained: you would select the most social species. They will be intelligent. They could attach markers & microphones. The Indian fruit bat is large & could carry weights & do heavy work. Bats could carry decorative flashing lights for displays at banquets. I wonder have circus people ever tried? You couldn't train a seagull but you could surely train a bat. I'm sure all cooperating animals can be trained & the more sophisticatedly they cooperate the better they can be trained. You can't really train a horse like you can train a dog but what would you train the bat to do?

The Simena boatyard
but the framing is wrong
vertical OK. Horizontal?

Salatin painting

Hasan fixing a bolt & nut

DEMEK = TO MEAN (or SAY)

SÖYLEMEK = To say

Vampires & fruit bats would be easier to feed than insect eaters. & I think vampires are very intelligent & social

We had lunch at the Deniz

Then in the afternoon Hassan Tülü took me with him on a shopping trip into Demre where I got a piece of board for doing cross paintings and a pair of trousers: thin cotton; pyjama; no flies; drawstring type for TL 7,000,000 @ £1 = 1,850,000 that's £3.78p: the price of a large gin & tonic in a smart hotel.

Smudge print with finger
then drawn with pen

better 'cos I have
used a separate much
weaker solution bottle
for the smudge

Today

Tilley

Roundstone Harbour

Roundstone Harbour

lunch @ The palmiye Monday
Proarte no. 5
4.6.2007
the bigger brush is better - more water hold = more mixing on the page

THURSDAY
LUNCH @ THE
PALMIYE. Delicious
Fresh fish (one each)

Wednesday   Nov. 5th 2008

Euphoria! because Obama got in as President of America
Joaquin is in Heaven

Monster secondary bank (merchant bank - or money gamblers) crisis. Lehman bros bankrupt. Merril Lynch also gone (taken over). 'Told you so' is of course the first reaction also 'good riddance'. Flashy gamblers high on wits and words - low on wisdom. We saw it coming: credit piled on credit in ever ever increasing heaps of inventive methods of lending which nobody really understood "Financial instruments" "Derivatives" Sub prime borrowings amalgamated, chopped up and traded (sold) on. New names for old tricks

Understandably people want blood but we won't get it.

tilley

TUESDAY feb 26 '13 Tree felling (pruning actually) at Boar's
bright sun, High Wind
Excellent Turkish proposal for a modern update of Islam
A sort of 'reformation' anounced yesterday
is badly needed!

midsummer flowers from Pat's border

RTE says "a woman in Scotland has become the first woman outside the Americas to have died of the H1N1 swine flu virus, but there is no cause for alarm 'course not!"

If you don't 'connect' you won't get anywhere

SUNDAY July 12th

My daemons seem to have evaporated – well a bit. The main thing is that I have managed to enlist helpers – mostly Anthony to sort out the admin. nightmare at D&W D&W Georgia is the problem + Anthony will jazz her up – I HOPE!! Then D&W will be merged into AD Ltd.

Thunder moon near 3rd ¼ overcast + spitting rain – a bit odd for midsummer

going to lunch with the HTs today

Coxed four in Mode 2 individuals fitting in together rules of unison apply, cox in charge

Today I'll make a start on the final magazine article. first sorting out modes. Make them plain & understandable with examples of rowing & definition

canal at Avondiff photo 18.8.09
boy fishing

THURSDAY

August 27th 2009

BMT

the moon should be looking like this but I haven't seen it yet

Final struggle (I hope) today with modes – are they real? logical even? What are they? alternative behavioural governing principles or phases through which every cooperator cycles. perhaps they are a set, a set, also, a set of governing principles

if I can solve this and it turns turns out to be complex it needn't actually go in the essay

Freya Alicia Wilson
2 months + 3 wks old

Thursday Nov 26th 2009

December 5th 2009

pigment/water been annoying me, I must be more masterful with it red is a disappointment but purple won't let me down

1. SOCIETY IS ABOUT COOPERATION
2. SOCIOLOGY IS ABOUT SOCIETY
3. SO SOCIOLOGY IS ABOUT COOPERATION

(or the other way round)

I seem to notice that writings on sociology pay little or no attention to COOPERATION despite the fact that all society is founded on it → Somehow cooperation is taken for granted

And this is well known to be unwise: biologists have known for 100 years that natural selfishness destroys cooperation at all levels of life and must be overcome

The mechanisms for doing this are also now understood: Q-sensing, caste systems & brainpower. Also Rb−c > 0 (add also my 3 mt)

So there seems to be a huge gap in sociology waiting to be filled by an understanding of the mechanisms of cooperation: in other words by three modes thinking

Wednesday Jan 6th
More snow than there's been
since we first came to Turleigh in 1987

January 12th 2010 In the bleak midwinter Barton bridge by the boathouse a very smart new fence is being installed right round the club grounds despite the frozen ground

from photo
13.1.10

view down the field
below Turleigh mill
where Tilley and I often walk
Did a nice Acrylic of This on 18.1.10

MONDAY JANUARY 18TH 2010

I'm hoping to hear from Lord May & Profs Abell and Frey some time This week. Yesterday I read David Inglis, Prof of Sociology, Aberdeen in The ~~AJSR BJS~~ BJS he says (I agree) that Ulrich Beck is wrong to claim that because of globalisation multi-national corporations & all that classical sociology is dead & buried. Inglis claims support in this from Tönnies. But Inglis makes mistakes which are shown up by 3 Mr. Tönnies' theme was to contrast family based society with business based society. But he did it intelligently, often understanding that the two are simultaneous so Beck is wrong But yes of course says Bart they are overlapping groups like rings on the surface of a pond

Tilley watching the snow from photo taken 13.1.10

SATURDAY Feb 13th 2010
Just sent explanatory note about the 3rd Transition and about game theory to Prof Peter Abell @ LSE Ireland v France in Paris. Today: big match between 1st & 2nd favourites.

TUESDAY feb 16th 2010 from The D.Telegraph 15.2.10 caption reads 'Lacrosse players jump for a ball during a match at Merton Abbey, 1923
Blue puton with Winter, Hat, fine hazy, No.3
I seem to be getting a cold

Find a Turkish radio station

SATURDAY Canal view from Elbow Cottage from photo 9.3.10
March 13th 2010 lovely heart warming event this morning two men in a white van noticed I had a puncture and realising I was old feeble & stupid they fixed it for me - charming

March 23rd 2010
Oscar being shy
from photo
21·3·10

Hoar frost this morning
phantom desire to pee at 2am
last night

 have moon

line get colour into it. start with
       drawing

10·5·10

I start this book in a spirit of optimism not just because I'm sitting on the balcony of room 5 Kalepansiyon, Kekova, Simena, Demre, Antalya, Turkey.

But also because of 2 recent advances ① discovering that putting on the first darks in gouache with a thick brush helps to connect properly with the page 'recte registrant' — and can then be made precise with a rigger nos. 0, 1 or 2. ② closing in on my latest essay on WALKLATE & MYTHEN'S paper in the march 2010 issue of the BJS about their key words: reflexivity, structure, agency, risk. (These words run wild. BUT can harness them into an ordering pattern using control loop concepts like scissors paper & stone. To show the dynamics of human social behaviour perpetually. (a) nested collection of myriad interacting groups. (b) these groups become & decay (form and decay). the quasi-mind of a group iterates round our control word

(in their paper and also in all contemporary sociology it seems)

tuesday
very windy
indeed
probably bringing dust
from the Sahara

May 23rd
2010

What happened yesterday? Well it was cold cold 26.66° in England that's 80°F colder here and COLD again this morning. Thick vest woolly hat and several layers. Thick red bed socks in bed. Let's hope that wind doesn't get up again today. And my painting yesterday was ugly.

Mosquitoes I've got a good technique with the mosquitos: I run Shower room whack em back hand with wet knuckles. For some reason they don't seem to be little able to escape the spatters & they don't bother me. Pee in the shower too! Pee in. & wee it's the peeing for.

"I'm on my mobile on the pier at the Pavilion where are you?"

THAT'S WHAT I WANT
I want to promote sociology that reflects the biology of our human/animal nature not pie in the sky socialism
THAT'S WHAT I WANT:
sociology not socialism

Yasin & Yufuk manoeuvring Kader out from its mooring spot
Wake-up drawings from yesterday's collected photos direct from camera window held in left hand

★ In the small Quai- mini RUMOURS, GOSSIP & MOODS → They can spread like wild-fire: The more people the more it spreads. They became impressed loose tongues & undisciplined. Nature's first law is to help society to help you, so dictator's that want to be so brutal didn't have to.

We gave Tine & Detlef dinner @ the pansiyon last night — went off well. We all had ORHAN'S BALIK SHISH. Very nice. Tine & Detlef doing a diet. Which is somehow linked to acupuncture — very German. Seems to work though.

exhausted on Yurdakule pier

oh pay no attention — he's harmless!

from photo 14.7.10
i New camera

Oscar 20.7.10

31.8.10

Dawn & Theo
watching weed clearance at the
Olympic site canal photo 26.8.10

16.7.10

Supposed to be Robin Cooke having a glass of wine in his conservatory 15.7.'10 (bit of a failure)

July 27th 2010

Overcast but v. warm almost ~~almost~~ muggy this morning

full moon yesterday the Thunder Moon

REJECTION
Rejection Rejection

My paper on Wallate & Huxley was rejected by the BJS yesterday of course I'm very disappointed but I'll have to pull myself together. They said it's "alternately too narrow or too broad" for them so it's more like an opinion- or thought-piece than an article for a scholarly journal

But I'll keep at it because there is a sort of mystery or gap - why do sociologists ignore Darwin & cooperation and what happened to the idea of applying cybernetic control loops in Sociology?

The rejection note (e-mail) is signed by Jacquie GAUNTLETT — marvellous name for the occasion!

fat man belly-up on sunbed

October 7th 2010

No moon — Next comes the harvest moon

Pat was depressed last night, says she wants to go home. In the dumps — not sure why. Weather's been nice. But the cooking's poor. She was cross about the meat in our Ét Sautée being tough. Says Salih does it cast and only buys cheap meat. Yasin defends Salih but the ON-UGUR in Üçağiz can produce good steak — so why can't Salih? We think the chef ORHAN isn't good enough and needs to be replaced next year. Viv + Ju-Ju going this morning. Tine went away for a week or more yesterday — Germany for memorial event for her brother. + then A/A with her sister.

TREVOR HOLDSWORTH — GKN — my boss from 1969-72 Died. Viv brought a copy of the TIMES from ÜÇAĞIZ yesterday — Monday oct 3rd and it had a full page obituary of him. He was a fine man. I had more respect and admiration for him than any others of my bosses. J Shanborough, John Williams + John Grieves. His obituary — written in a dull sycophantic industrialist PR hand. Fails to do him justice. Doesn't catch his wit, humour + light touch. In the industrial Midlands he was a star amongst full 'iron master' worshipers. He was 83 — young to die. I wonder how he died.

SATURDAY 23rd Oct 2010   **MICK DOES A RUNNER!**

Mick has gone a day early without saying goodbye. Amazing WE'RE STUNNED. We watched Ersin take him in the dinghy to ÜÇAĞIZ. He sat there with 2 big bags, went past our pier, didn't look over. Must have known Pat & I were sitting there at the closest point sitting looking forward he studiously put on his glasses. Avoiding any chance of a glance. He knew he hates saying goodbye so we sat there quiet as mice. Was he getting away from us? If wasn't the weather because it's an idyllic beautiful windless, blue-sky morning. Had he thought he'd told us too much last night. Criminal past? or what? Were we getting too close? Will we ever see him again? The innocent explanation that he always intended to leave today & just didn't tell us 'cos he hates goodbyes.

November 1st 2010
back i Turleigh
after 5 wks i
Slovenia.

overcast, cold
gloomy, damp

a little the worse for wear
but optimistic in mood

The worse for wear because Pat's back is not getting any better and the journey home aggravates it. Also I still have a very sore knee after falling 2 wks ago of Tine's boat. Then as well That delightful puppy Maira ate my mobile phone, glasses and hearing aid.

Luke + Krysta came to see us yesterday which was very nice. They have a new car - Krysta's dad - and new floor i their downstairs rooms.

Freddie fell and was in tears briefly he went to Oscar to get a cuddle of comfort. Freddie 2½ Oscar 4½ never seen that before. Krysta + Luke were right there as well: it was very sweet

SUNDAY NOVEMBER 14th 2010

D Hunter's moon

Luke + family coming to lunch today 7.10am Pat's just put a slow cooking huge T-Bone joint of beef in the oven. I'll get Luke to help me with brewing. I want his help cos I'm not keen to put too much effort into my poor left knee which is still sore + aching after that fall in Sumava.

My efforts now are all on finishing 3rd paper submission to the BJS. I'm thinking of renaming it "HOW SOCIETY WORKS" or "Society - how it works" something like that. BUT I do feel I'm getting old, as I said to Thomas on the phone yesterday I'm beginning to realise that I'm not going to go on living forever.

And another complaint: I caught myself becoming English yesterday, rather shocking. Was watching England v Australia on TV up @ the Rugby club where they have SKY TV - we don't. It was a terrific match + a great win for England 35-18. But towards the end I was desperate for England to win, and at Twickenham. I mean for goodness sake what sort of a Norman Tebbitt's come over me?

December 13th 2010

Weather gloomy but a little bit warmer. Saw the moon yesterday it must have been my first view of the Long Night moon. Today at last I feel a bit more optimistic — positive (modern word) about my leg — left ankle. I'll start painting in Acrylics again today — A portrait of Theo methinks. Pete & Jill have gone they were here for 2½ weeks. It was lovely to have them to stay — but its also nice to have the house back to ourselves again.

TINKER, TAILOR, SOLDIER, SAILOR
RICHMAN, POORMAN, BEGGARMAN, THIEF

Who you are. I've been thinking how what you do in life shapes who you are. Doctors are like doctors they develop a sort of caring kindness — sure of themselves socially. Accountants shut ideas down. They respect facts above all else & so are two dimensional lacking imagination — not willing to explore ideas. Airline pilots are constantly on the verge of break-out rather like long term prison inmates. It takes little to get them going. After all they are only highly paid bus drivers. So there's a warning here for youngsters setting out on lifes journey: an indication of what'll happen to you. And your personality as by Theo years go by.

You will become what you do Tinker, Tailor, Soldier, Sailor, Richman, Poorman, Beggarman, Thief. There's a moving pictures facility on my new zoom camera which I want to learn about. I've just discovered it!

You'll fill your brain up over the years AND it's up to you what you put in it

A man Thing   TUESDAY 21st.
SHORTEST DAY & LUNAR ECLIPSE

Depression?

The carefree young man has time on his hands. He messes about. Gets married. Takes the business of making money more + more seriously. Without noticing he works harder. Some say he's become a workaholic. No more spare time.

Like most other men I've been buzzing about — not making money now that I'm retired but painting, writing, rowing, sculpting. Doing and making.

I frequently wonder what would happen if I stopped. Afraid that if I don't keep swimming I'll drop to the sea floor and die.

Well, doing nil for the past 3 weeks because of my broken leg, I think I've now found out: The erstwhile workaholic who stops gets depressed. DEPRESSED. Very simple really. Not clinically depressed of course but nevertheless deprived of the will to live.

Two solutions — ① Snap out of it by making things again
                ② Try to find to the carefree Pre-workaholic life — rediscover it

I suppose the clever thing is to find a wavelength between ① & ②

That must be what they mean when they talk about growing old gracefully — But how d'ya do that??

Went out on crutches to feed the pigeons this morning. New shower tray just goes in. The workers got here despite the treacherous roads.

So that's a huge load off my mind

JAN 4th 2011

The lovely view from my bed
— my very comfy bed

Doctors 866611
Winsley H. Centre
↳ 860003
Appointments 865200
Home visits 860018
Out of Hours service 01249 456530
Health Visitors 865660
District Nurses 863782
Social Services 867795

If God had intended us to draw
he'd have given us one eye
not two — but my new
BIFOCAL glasses are good for
near & far

Tuesday Jan 4th 10.36 am

in bed — leg in plaster & suffering from "weakness
after slightest effort" coughing up muck at regular
intervals. And with leg in plaster. Can't get
through to the doctors but don't want to as I
feel a flu'y coming — going to cancel Paul
and the mag next weekend

my brewing bin etc. photo 18-2-11

moon of 3rd past full

February 21st 2011
we've decided after MUCH debate that we will have a joint 80th birthday party with Derek on May 2nd Pat wasn't keen but we've talked her round

weather heavily overcast: the clouds must be a mile deep or more.

I'm writing up my '3-MT' paper for submission to the journal called Philosophy of the Social Sciences (PSS) PSS it is American, highly ranked by SJR and published recent papers by Anthony King, Nimrod Bar-am and Mouelamo Tuomela — all very similar to 3-MT

RAIMO

I'm starting new colours Today 2.3.11 or rather using a carefully selected set of 12 Watercolours + some Gouaches — mostly W+N. See p 97 last page of previous sketchbook.

Select colours direct — no mixing using wide hogshair spade brush about 14mm plus (after colour washes) drawing with bamboo stylus

Theo in Victoria park

POPPER   Karl Popper said that for an hypothesis to be regarded as scientific it needs to be falsifiable and if it ever is falsified it must immediately be rejected — 3-MT is falsifiable. → abandoned

Tithe barn interior photo 6.3.11

find a stylus inset method

March 6th 2011
I'm excitedly cooking up the necessary and sufficient argument for 3-ht of course I may well fail

Robin & Charlotte Cooke are about to arrive for Dinner to fix Sinews dates for next mon

Har mon
V cold & raw weather

March 27th 2011

So what is the question — That's the real question. Just finishing 'An Evening of long goodbyes' by Paul Murray. Terrific writer. I think I'll send a copy to John Gibson by Amazon. He spends long boring hours at hospital these days undergoing kidney dyalisis. I'm trying to calm down after the great crescendo — a clashing of cymbals in my head — finishing my paper 'Co-operation: a Three modes theory of social dynamics'. Sent it off (America spelling) Monday last 21st Apr to the PSS. Calming down means dealing with Insurance, holiday bookings (Simeiza in May) And getting back my painting head. For this I'm doing a detailed panorama of Turleigh from the Dam.

Hare moon in its last ¼. Rain moon is next. Then Blossom, Thunder & honey. Current high pressure weather. Clock change today brings SUMMER

↑ Dr Nigel Gough (60) our GP + Leslie. Nigel is a very competent family doctor. Senior partner at our local practice. Knows us all + the village rather intimately which somewhat cramps his style at village parties. Leslie is difficult to know but nice.

↑ Derek (Dr) & Anne Heap (80) our closest village friends — the ones we go drinking + pub lunching with. Derek is 1wk older than me

↑ (75) Susan Bacon (70) lives on her own — slight mental problems (schitzophrenia?)

David & Nicola Cope (55) live below us in Turleigh with small adopted son James. Nice people.

↑ Roger Bertrand (78) retired journalist, bit of an intellectual snob, lives on his own

↑ Anna Tain (73) swedish aristocrat V. beautiful, lives alone

Mike + Beth McCoy-Hill (85) grumpy now social but nice some tragedy in their past

Turleigh Cottage Pat (75) & me (80)

Anna is divorced from multi-millionaire John Tain. They used to live in TURLEIGH MANOR. She is fey (not to say away with the fairies)

March 28th 2011

Half moon waxing

'UPLANDS'
John & Janice Short
Rower @ BOARC
(55) businessman
pleasant but stalker

The Allens (63)
Jean & Martin
nice people

Turleigh Manor
Pat & Geraldine NG
Pat & geraldine anti-social
Chinese — The Grand house

Nice weather — very nice
mornings cold & frosty

Turleigh Panorama drawn from memory

Mark & Helen
Farmer (55)(45)
@ The Malt House
nice neighbours
lots of self-made money
toys (cars, small planes etc)

James & Candida
McNeile (43) Pair
at The Close. Superficially
pleasant but Lawyers
& aggressive. They annoy
everybody with an elbows out
policy about property.

Bob Pratt + Clare (43)
nice but not
V social. Bob is a
builder — big handsome
strong man — vague.

Brian & Martha
Michlau. She's
French. V. nice
people (70) She's
petite he's a retired
merchant navy captain

Doug who has horses
& goes to Bath
rugby — has a season
Tkt. (60)

Monday continues here.
Strange still unreal feel to the morning. Clocks changed yesterday so it is
6.27 but till 2 days ago it would have been 7.27 am
At least I'm fully fit again — no aches, pains or tiredness
(not much anyway) after yesterday's sculling outing. The trip
it has taken me about 2 mths — has been a great help

At BOARC
CRICKET — The one-day world cup
Tournament — semi-final against England
Sri-Lanka (Ceylon) England made
made 230 all out
SRI LANKA 231 without
LOSING A WICKET

Wednesday May 4th ~~2010~~ 2011

Off to SIMENA tomorrow but we've had a busy time. The main thing was the joint birthday party we gave on Monday for Derek + me — both 80!

New blossom moon — very dry now. The high weather continues but it's colder.

Paul came to stay 3 nights (Sat, Sun + Mon) pompous as ever but he is an integral part of our lives & we love him. Getting married he says to Lesley Kennedy, but "The details still have to be worked out" — That's putting it mildly. She wants to stay in America, he wants to pass the widow's portion of his substantial pension to somebody. But it is a romantic match. She's coming over in June but not to England & she's not going to meet his friends or family. Things being pulled her way by some sort of selfish gravity. Is he throwing too many temptations + concessions her way carelessly? We're nervous about it, and very much hope it works. One problem is she wants to keep her USA job & so will only get short holidays every year. Much/most in USA we fear.

On Monday May 2nd.
The party was a great success largely thanks to Jemima Penrose who did the catering, friend of Krysta, highly professional and nice person. She had 3 helpers incl. her cousin Sue. She did several excellent things. Best was to arrange 2 trestle tables in front of the work surfaces in the front kitchen. The tables, end to end, allowed a work place for Jemima + helpers to serve food arranged in the back kitchen before being carried round. They also thus had the sink cupboards + cooker right there when wanted.

39 people invited. Roger Berthoud forgot to come. Also Mark + Luke + Dawn + Krysta brought their little children Oscar, Theo, Freddie + Freya who added nicely to the event playing round the pond + generally 'imp-ing' about. Extremely well behaved. No tears or anything.

Buffet lunch was excellent. 2 courses + then cheese + coffee. Some of the Heaps' friends not quite our choice. But never minds because it was a JOINT PARTY celebrating both Derek's & my 80th birthdays.

Jemima charged ~~£~~ £24.00 per head = £936.00 8
MINES Leisure hire supplied plates, glasses, cutlery, folding chairs, trestle tables (2) + lots of sundry things. They will charge separately.

The guest list was our special old friends & the Marsh & Lake families plus village people (several left out) & some odd Heap friends. See above p52 for the story about why the Reeves' didn't come. + Jacky Reeves then played the fishwife about parking.

What made the party extra good was the way Jemima waved the people around. Nice weather. 1. Drinks on arrival on the terrace outside. Then people streamed in via the hall, some via the conservatory. To help themselves at the trestle tables. Actually Jemima + Sue served them. + Then they found places to sit – the drawing room. Kitchen dining room – Conservatory end. Conservatory or outside. Outside was best. Lots sat on chairs etc. outside.

Invitation was for 12:00. Food served at 1:00 & by 4 pm many had gone. + Jemima + her team left at 4 pm having cleared everything away but not washed or rinsed it. She also took a black plastic bag full of rubbish. Next day I rinsed + counted everything that had to go back to theirs. They came + collected at 1:30 p.m. next day.

People sat around outside about 10 of us till about 6 p.m. Oscar, Theo, Freddy & Fraser threaded themselves in + out of the party like quicksilver. Oscar proudly gave me a Sturgeon for the pond: a Sterlet. It was christened Sir Lobster.

As parties go it was an enjoyable + successful event. Gilly & Pete + Paul stayed the night. Made a Dawn drove back to London. Leaving at 7:00 p.m.

Our special old friends were: Delaps, Gilly + Pete, Paul, Hatvanys, Brewers, HILL

So how do you feel Tony now that you're 80? people ask. Well I feel very well really, inside myself: still rowing, maybe a bit slow, but still the same me. No change. But then in the car coming up to the T-junction at the witches' house (Masons'?) – BOA I forgot to put my indicator to turning left. A man coming across my bows from New Barn to go up Mason's hill could have gone on but didn't know I was turning left. He wound down his window and shouted at me "You silly old fool straight at him yes, he said, old. But I don't feel like that – not really.

May 8th 2010 Simena

Today I'll face the music. Got an e-mail on Friday rejecting my paper - that is from PSS (Philosophy of the Social Sciences) it came with 7 pages of notes from the peer reviewers who read it. I was so disappointed, and of course also interrupted by the journey here, that I didn't look at it.

Blossom moon but weather fresh, just not quite cold. Been a cold spring they say

on May 5th Today we flew to Dalaman

May 26th 2011

The other reason why I'm glad that god didn't "gie us the giftie to see ourselves as others see us" (Rob't Burns - see yesterday) is that if we did, self criticism would stifle creativity. I always say that if there is any gift which an artist is born with it's the belief that anything you make is better than it really is. So you think your painting is wonderful and the thrill you get [thus] makes you repeat it again & again narcissistically - with the constant repetition you do actually get better & better - it's inevitable. So thank goodness the power didn't "the giftie giftie gie me." Father said of Thomas "he always thinks his geese are swans" but I now understand that Thomas is lots more successful jokes on father because father who became disappointed as a painter - although he had great "talent" early on - it was never really fulfilled.

Blossom moon is high in sky which is overcast this morning

Wednesday 25th   THE POWER AND THE GIFTIE   7

Did I mention 'oh would the power the giftie gie us'
The ode to a mouse I think it is by Robt. Burns? Later: No it's
                                                  to a slug on
Well there are two excellent (reasons) why I thank god that a ladies'
                                                   bonnet — the
he didn't. The First (is) that I'd much rather not see few — but
myself as others see me: a silly old fool, boring, slightly (damn it
deaf, slow on the uptake, forgetful, clumsy & altogether) churned
feeble, white-haired & bent. I much happier with the
intelligent, upright, sharp-minded, sprightly person I
think myself to be.   PTO for the second reason

lunch at
the Palmiye

May 28th 2011
Manchester Utd.
V. Barcelona in the
European Cup final Today

Blossom
moon shines
its 2011
goodbye in a faintly-
cloudy sky - it is v.
warm

Poor Pat is in agony
a slipped disc I think at
the joint above where her
spine was fused about 5 yrs
ago. It came on yesterday morning & got
worse as the day progressed — no dinner, no
lunch yesterday and no wine or Raki last night.
I'v given her sleeping pills & she slept quietly last
night. Not up yet. **PAT IN AGONY** it
Luke + family seems to be that awful pain that
screeches through your central nervous
system — indescribable
canoeing and swimming

May 30th 2011
Luke + Krysta's
last day here -
they go home
tomorrow Mustafa
is taking them in his
big car

No moon
Honeymoon
on Wednesday - Pat's
birthday. Dull &
overcast today, spots
of rain. Damp - my towel
didn't dry last night — I
hang it out to dry every
night beside my bed on the
balcony

THE DIARY/SKETCHBOOK →
Now why've I written that?
Who'm I telling?

**GOD IS MY SKETCHBOOK AND
VICE-VERSA**

Not myself because I know it already
and nobody else because this diary/sketchbook isn't for
anybody else to read.
Bit of a puzzle really, like one of those philosophical riddles
UNLESS - this must be it - unless I'm telling my sketchbook
'Talking' to it. Like saying my prayers.
And the thing is that as I told Robin Cooke, if you're
honest it does sometimes tell you things. Like
saying your prayers — at least that's what the clergymen
sometimes say — or they did when I was at Eton.
And I have indeed found that my sketchbook or
my sketchbook writing sessions does and do sometimes
produce ideas — not necessarily answers to questions
but answers to questions I didn't know I was asking
— I didn't know I was asking

October 26th 2011

No moon this morning otw moon is next

DIS^sA^pPOINTMENT

Prof Anthony King of Exeter University has completely ignored my A+PT stuff — no response to my NLT (navigation Loop Theory) paper sent Sept 10 (approx) and no reply at all; silence total silence, after I sent him my interpretation of his CUBC 2007 draft article to go in the Dec 2011 issue of the BJS. What should I do?

At least get him to tell me he's got my interpretation ~~response to~~ CUBC 2011? → simple message? "Did you get the E-mail I sent on 10.10.11 about CUBC 2007?

Go down to Exeter in a cold call and sit on his doorstep? Go to one of his lectures? (security?) Go to Exeter Rowing Club? Is there one?

No: don't be a pest or a stalker.

one of our ducks is missing
the white one
sitting on eggs?
they used to go doing the rounds of the village in a little group of three
Now there are only two.

my T-bar-strap sandals

At home
Get an iPad for photos & reading
Make up daily acrylic sketch binder
devise a way to show A4 acrylics on mirrors
        (cheap flexible & exchangeable)

November 27th 2011
Long night moon coming up

Weather calm + dry. Mostly overcast high pressure weather.

Feeling better at last this morning I'll go down to BOARC and offer myself for cooking. The club is very short of cooks.

Pat on the phone to Mark who had rung to ask about her high blood pressure. OK she said but was raised by the excitement of the delivery + installation of new oven and hot-plate. Mark is very thoughtful

2 girls rigging their
double at BOARC
Lucy and that chinese
girl

Friday April 27th 2012
2 struggles going on buying Philly a house i Greystones
and sending off A&PT as submission of manuscript to BSS
still nobody reads it understands it or engages with it
meanwhile Tilley has arthritis & pain I've got the latest
version of glucosamine for her from the vet — my
rugby friend Roger Harrisson

November 26th 2021 8:38

Green eyes
Brown hair
Hormones out of balance

November 30th 2021
7:50

Beaver moon B
Waning crescent
it about 10%? Sky guide as usual is dubious

6:52

4:04
= 9: (-50 + 04)
= 8:14 Daylight hrs Today.

Lovely — very lovely visit from Vanessa yesterday. She cleaned the... she helped to reorganise my Denmitri's studio prompting with several good ideas — especially setting up the double decker table. We told each other stories & had hugs throughout. She gave me one tiny kiss. — Kisses are banned between us — I said "We're that a little kiss? She said well it won't happen again anyway nobody's the wiser. I told her that's the price she has to pay for her amazing vitality: lesser beings have lesser hormone imbalances. Tidying books I came across The Tiny book of "by-lines" by Niel O'Kennedy (?) cartoonist at the Irish Times in the 1950's. It included — started with — 3 of The Bowl of Light, so I told her the full story. She explained Brad's worry that he might not pass the annual Health Test. The one he must take to retain his HGV licence — he drives those heavy giant lorries. She described her work as a carer at Homestead.

January 22nd 2013
Deep winter morn
ice + snow everywhere
are open
Still ½ asleep
kids Today
hear

weather very cold
driving on the roads
but roads Treacherous. And I'm
getting 2 new hearing
that'll be good because there's lots I can't

good likeness here

Vanessa is a
ray of sunshine
She comes Monday
mornings and is
wonderfully lively
and vigorous she
sings as she works
the hoover & broom

Vanessa our very cheerful
and attractive cleaning lady,
She was recommended to us by Ella
when Ella stopped to have a baby;
Laura who is now 1 yr old

March 22nd 2013 The weather is NASTY. I went Hare moon for a cycle ride yesterday down to Avoncliff via Belcombe and back round by elbow cottage. It was freezing cold in the biting wind

going into a bad patch. Pat's not recovering and my art is becalmed. Don't want to say going through a bad patch 'cos he may never come out the other side = best not to tempt providence

I think the problem with my "Painter's block" is that I'm not approaching my "Oeuvre" seriously enough (no change there!) its a fine balance between inspired and frightened NEXT SWITCH PAGES, meaning to colour splash a RT page to be close to w. colours. SATURDAY's splash wed

SATURDAY March 23rd 2013

Etasy! Kath grainger & Anna Watkins won Gold in the Olympic double sculls. August 2012

19th of August 2013 — Barley Mow Wearyford HIKE

The big thing this week is going to be trying to get Pat's driving license back

+ Lunch @ The HT's today

+ Yesterday LtK came round for Tea with Oscar + Freddie

+ Mo Farah won the 10,000 And the 5,000 meters at the World Championships in Moscow a truly magnificent "Double" which he also did at the London Olympics last year making him one of the greatest

It's definitely in here somewhere I know it is — it's got to be

August 22nd 2013
Barley Moon
Dog Gise +

Daler "Dalon" requires a delicate touch — don't we all — and a two finger and thumb grip. Nice visit to the Cookes yesterday evening. They invited us to "tea at 4" followed by drinks at 6:horay civilised formula lots of chat as usual when we get together with them

Pat has had her driving license revoked on account of incipient dementia confirmed to the DVLA by Fackerell + Gough. She feels quite capable to drive and is upset about it. Me? Well I'm not surprised — she certainly isn't right but it's nasty to be 'fingered' in this way.

6.08 pm Just come back in. Pat fast asleep and looking very peaceful + calm. Mouth wide open breathing very steadily.

Karin Godoy phoned at lunch time. I was at home. She told me Joaquin had died on Friday. She + Jean-Pierre helped him put his pyjamas on + put him into bed + he died. Quick + simple.

JOAQUIN

DIED he was 89 a stout survivor despite his emphysema. We loved him. As I was speaking to Karin I had a just opened letter from him in front of me. The post mark was Nov 29th Friday last, the day he died.

DISASTER

MY HOPE NOW IS THAT THE ENGLISH HAVE VOTED IT WILL LEAD TO TO LEAVE THE EU THE UNIFICATION OF IRELAND

WOE AND WAIL

5.59 Pat fast
asleep again
sleep is good for her
to re-make the
connections
Luke'll be here
shortly he was
just waiting for
Oscar to get back
from chess club

There's a man - NURSE
nurse on
tonight. A nice chap

that's
enough
Hospital
scenes
for now AND
TIME FOR SOME
COLOUR

Nurse is incompetent
and Pat's a terrible
coward. Pat's still
full y blonde at
78!

RUTH Midford ward
last week. Nurse failing
to get blood from vein
Pat's arm

Monday April 14th The hare moon is full + Pat is dead
Terrible words. The Truth is Terrible
Some times.

This morning when I woke I felt what the hell? Let it all go

But that's wrong I have lovely children & grandchildren and lovely friends and Pat was a wonderful wonderful person she was me or part of me + I was part of her.

I can see that writing down my thoughts + events will keep me afloat.

Next to set up SKYPE to communicate with Mark + the children

But next I must continue the narrative on Page 92 above where I left it — No writing yesterday Sunday because Mark was here + Luke came and I was stunned.

From: **Home1** tony.wilson678@gmail.com
Subject: to John. Sad news
Date: 14 April 2014 09:46
To: r. john gibson gibson rjgibson@nf.sympatico.ca

Dear John,

Desperately sad: Pat died on Friday. It was sudden but I'd been expecting something to happen. Her health was deteriorating. Beginnings of alzheimers and not at all steady walking etc.

She was all there, tottered out for a rare shopping trip with me the day before, cooked a lovely stew that evening.

Next morning she bent down to straighten a rug in front of the fire; terrific pain and off to the hospital in an ambulance. She had torn her aorta but at the time I thought it wasn't serious and that they'd fix her up quickly; didn't realise. I was stunned when the doctor and nurse came out of the CT scan room to tell me that she has stopped breathing and had no pulse. You mean you're telling me she's dead I said. I'm terribly sorry he said. And that was it. All over. 5hrs from the pain till she died.

I'm ripped apart between piercing sorrow wondering what it must actually, really have been like for her. Feeling sad and sorry for myself. And responsible, needing to respect and soothe the emotions of those who loved her. Mostly Mark, Philly and Luke. But also lots of others. When they try to console me I think selfishly of myself and then realise guiltily that they too are upset and deeply saddened. I need to console them.

Pat as you well know was forthright sometimes to the point of being downright rude. But people seemed to forgive her that, some even enjoyed the truth telling. And she was much loved by those who knew her. A real personality. I know you and Judy were very fond of her.

It's all very raw right now. I'll be OK. funeral arrangements now starting. Funeral probably in the week of Monday April 28th.

lots of love to you both, Tony

TUESDAY April 15th 12.35 am   94

[sketch of full moon] full moon

Derek has just gone back to Yorkshire (Nunthorpe). Pat's death affected him a lot. He was cheerful/gloomy.
I'm alone now but Luke's coming — He's been a huge help. Then at 2.30 Denize from Bowyers The undertakers comes.
I feel sad. Then I wonder why. Then I remember + Think OH FUCK! it happens on + off just when I've got into a calm patch of normality.
But Poor Pat. Poor pat what about her? What was it like? **FOR HER?**

YESTERDAY

"Derek + I went to see Pat's body — The Mortuary (euphemistically "The chapel of rest". I met him off The Train in Bath. + We went in together. Very nice lady Suzanne Dale There. I took photos. Pat looked Very Beautiful. Heartwrenchingly beautiful.

Wednesday 16th.

I can hear her Telling me "you stupid bugger" wondering what it was like for her (5 hours after They told me she had died) what it was like for her actually dying — it opened up a black hole a void. Then did she have a soul or what. That brought me (MISERY) beyond science + philosophy to a realm of mistery + I realised That That's what the church is all about. Christian, Islam, every religion. So though we were not church goers we were Most definitely christian + I bend my knee to This church and all it stands for

and we were most certainly not atheists or humanists we were christian

8.25 pm Lucinda phoned earlier today and said a good Thing: that life comes in boxes. You close one and then you open another — good; That! A new phase of My life will open up she means and she's right

9.19 pm Talking to Krysta who is at Wenhall and also earlier to Lucinda. I realise that married couples push each other around or bully each other mercilessly and That's the way its got to be. The Trick is to Reach an equilibrium

THURSDAY April 17th 2014

Sad. Desperately, piercingly sad.
I thought I was getting over it yesterday
when Lucinda told me over the phone
about Life Coming in Bates. See p 94 above
She's right — BUT I'm not ready to see if there's another but +
if there is: not ready to open it

A HANDFULL   Pat was a handful — more on equilibrium...
She was gifted with beauty, quick repartee, a
simple + direct philosophy and a super memory.
All good weapons to push me around with.
(don't talk to me about syntax etc) not perhaps
push me around as keep me in line 'on the
straight & narrow'.
That way all married couples come to their
equilibrium — sometimes a strange one. Think of
partners in crime, + other weirdos. It's a sort of
'mutual bullying'. Pat and I kept that balance O.K.

Gone for ever but what was it like? Just oh oh
here we go + then nothing? What was it like? What
were the final moments actually like? Where did she
go + what was it she that went? Now alive, now
dead? These thoughts ~~~~~~~~ lead directly to
the place occupied by religion where some people, not
Pat & me, worship god. We didn't but we were
Christians, not Atheists or humanists, druids or
anything

They've made me President of BoARC. I'm
flattered and feel loved But Not without
a hiccup: Very dear Jim Brown — father of 3
hotshot oarsmen, past captain + extremely
same... quiet nice chap had been nominated
by Carl Purchase, outgoing chairman, as his
successor. The committee decided No to that
but that leaves poor Jim potentially pissed off.
I'll delicately find out about that.

Sketchbook repairs: They keep falling apart at the binding
Maybe I should use binder clips for (egg) dev
And: Maybe I shouldn't use foldbacks clips to glue

Pat's tree
Sequoyadendron giganteum
Photographed by Oliver who
was keen to get the house
in the background. One day
soon the tree will hide the
house in this view

IT'S NEW YEAR'S DAY

and I'm thinking "What the hell — what's the point?" I wish Pat were still alive. I do miss her so much. The answer I know is to stop thinking about myself, but that's easy to say. The real answer is to do and make things. I remember saying to Pat, when we were wondering if we should get married, that though I was well qualified and could always earn well as a Chartered Accountant, that my dream has always been to paint + sculpt, and that one day I hoped to retire after we had brought up a family and paint. She didn't reply but of course we got married and had children, but she did remember my self-indulgent and pathetic dream. Well Now I can chase it. I will and I must. That's the answer to my "What the hell?" question. Of course I'm a bit old, but the single-minded focus is the thing. Also I do now have got rid of my Assembly & Performance thinking. I've done it. Spewed it out. It will probably land with a dull thud like a liquid cow-pat flopping onto the grass, but that's that. ⟶ splat - splat.

January 1st 2017
deep winter moon

Yesterday Oliver came with me to watch Exeter beat Bath, because Hughie was ill & a bit. couldn't come. Oliver's not a bit interested in rugby but realising I'd be lonely all on my own he came to keep me company.

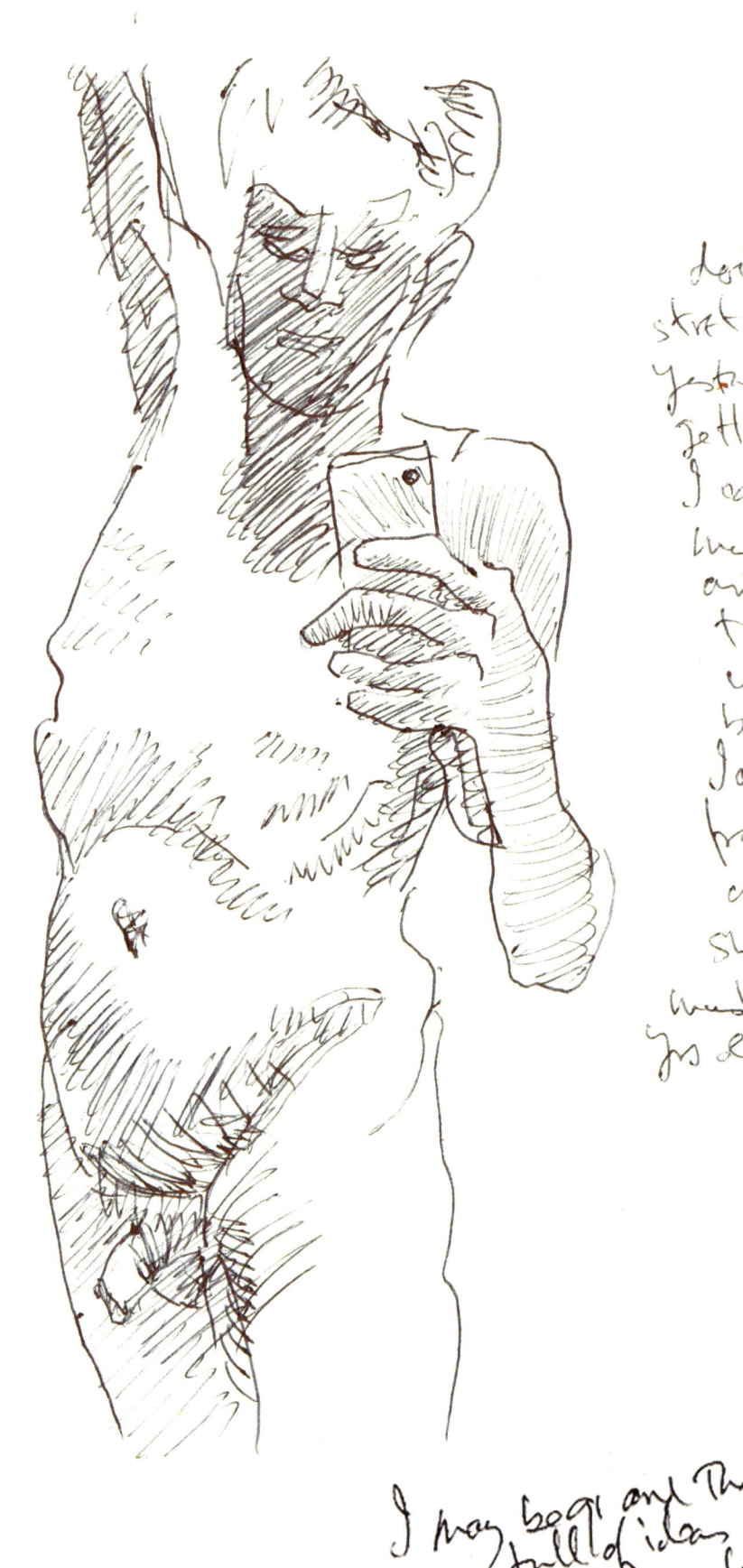

doing some stretching exercises yesterday before getting in the shower I caught sight of myself in the mirror and was shocked to see what a wretched looking bundle of bones I am — far removed from my own conception of myself — rather shocking. I am, it must be admitted, 83 yrs old but still

my head is full of ideas esp about space time + the Cosmos at human scale that I'm afraid I'll never get them all out. And then there are space-time panos & space-time modelling. is there another book there?? must ask grace what she thinks